Some Heaven

Some Heaven

POEMS by TODD DAVIS

Michigan State University Press • *East Lansing*

⊗ The paper used in this publication meets the minimum require-
ments of ANSI/NISO Z39.48-1992 (R 1997) (Permanence of Paper).

 Michigan State University Press
East Lansing, Michigan 48823-5245
www.msupress.msu.edu

Printed and bound in the United States of America.

13 12 11 10 09 08 07   1 2 3 4 5 6 7 8 9 10

LIBRARY OF CONGRESS CATALOGING-IN-PUBLICATION DATA
Davis, Todd F., 1965–
Some heaven : poems / by Todd Davis.
p. cm.
ISBN-13: 978-0-87013-800-3 (pbk. : alk. paper)
ISBN-10: 0-87013-800-6 (pbk. : alk. paper)
I. Title.
PS3604.A977S66 2007
811'.6—dc22
2006100334

Book and cover design by Sharp Des!gns, Inc.
Cover artwork is "The Great Piece of Turf" by Albrecht Dürer and is
used courtesy of the Albertina, Vienna.

g green Michigan State University Press is a member of the Green
  press Press Initiative and is committed to developing and en-
  INITIATIVE couraging ecologically responsible publishing practices. For more in-
formation about the Green Press Initiative and the use of recycled paper
in book publishing, please visit *www.greenpressinitiative.org.*

Visit Michigan State University Press on the World Wide Web at
www.msupress.msu.edu

Contents

1

2

3

4

Some Heaven

For Shelly, Noah, and Nathan

1

The Possibility of Rain

Late August, yet farmers are already in their fields.
Rain hasn't fallen since June, leaving us nothing
but the harvest: beans hard as bbs, cornstalks brittle
as bone in the wake of summer's relentless heat.
As I drive home through the dark, I see the fires
have begun—sparks from combines to blame.
I pull out of the way of the sirens that wail on
into the growing black, smoke billowing
from the field to the back of Yoder's barn.
These men who come from town know
such conflagrations will build toward heaven
despite their best efforts. But who among us
can stop believing in the possibility of rain?
Dust rises from gravel roads with our nervous
movement, our need to work, and then catches
in the backs of our throats. For the past three
weeks, each night we wake and walk barefoot
through tall grass, heavy dew brushing the inside
of our thighs. An entire town up an hour before
daybreak, hiking toward the western skyline
where we believe thunderheads build, great
bellies of rain that promise something better
but only leave us miles from home.

Home

Does the wind grow tired? Does the river ever stop
and flow back the way it has come? Does the vireo's throat
need rest, or the heron's neck ache? Why do we spend so much
of what is given to us in complaint and argument? The parasite
burrows beneath the skin of a maple, yet the tree does not lament
its bad luck, bend its trunk in grief. Instead it begins the slow growth:
bole's bulge to bleed out or seal over this possible death, which years
from now will begin to decay. In that place and time, again, no grievance,
only the pleasure that in this death some other life will make a home.

After Jamie Wyeth's "New Growth" (1971)

What We Have Heard Carried Upon the Wind

Corn grows tall here—no elephant's eye
needed to measure it, to understand
how our fields sprawl, acre upon acre
tiled, drained, folded back and forth
like the sick flesh in the pictures
we pored over in sixth grade, the yellowed
pages of the health book where we learned
to say *elephantiasis*—how bizarre
and removed from us it seemed: legs
that surely could not be legs, bodies bloated
like balloons that would no longer float,
like the drowned that were dragged from the river
during the big flood our grandparents remembered.

During recess we whispered so the teacher
would not catch us talking about how
the doctors carved the excess, what we thought
was done with the skin, how it might grow back
together into something else. I wonder now
if it's the same as dredging the great river
that cuts the heart of this country in two?
Layer after layer of the land's body flying up
into the air, farm legs growing thinner
with each year, plows sending top soil east
with the wind, toward a far-off land
where the dark-skinned still walk
on elephant's legs.

Amish Gardens

Toward the middle of September when late flowers
bloom and orange and red peppers dangle close

to chrysanthemums, the yellow squash and last zucchini
tangle, full hips writhing like new lovers caught

in pumpkin vines, the bold orange of their pregnant bellies
taking over everything. Here the order she worked hard

to cultivate through the unruly summer gives ground
to the growing season's final days, and she wonders

what might lurk under these large, green leaves; what exactly
was lost when we left the garden long ago. Little time

remains to tend to such matters, harvest hard upon her.
Yet she is bothered by the brightness of these last blossoms,

the way their mouths pout at the very thought of the first
hard frost—earth moist from melting cold, plow pushing it

all safely under, garden bed as dark and rich as her husband's
thighs hidden beneath plain trousers.

For Elsie and David Kline

Penance

There are still towns in the Midwest where the men grow
eight feet and taller, shoulders wide, back muscles held
like so many full baskets of bread, skin in summer as tan

as its crusts. And in these towns where the only scales
are found at the feed store, men and women cut the fields
by hand, blades swung through in swaths as wide

as basswood trunks, wheat shocks bunched like flowers,
and hay put to rest in lofts with pitch forks. Here the only
thing sacred is sowing and reaping: thick fingers grasp

wooden staves as in prayer, arms sway to the earth
then the heavens, with the same devotion as their fathers
and their fathers' fathers, who dug ditches across

the rolling flat, tiled fields, laid down new rivers and roads
upon a prairie where Indians quickly became ghosts. So many
Christian soldiers drunk on loss and sorrow and the shining pride

of a people who believed first in order and then discipline,
who in the worst snows send their young out into the storm
to shovel their streets, their highways that run toward

the horizon's blank stare, winds blowing snow and soil sideways,
drifts mounting like buffalo, boys and girls learning that this is how
they grow strong: straight white teeth bared, blond hair falling

forward, the serene beauty of their long limbs as they toss
the snow into the fields with a righteousness that must be paid for
and a strength that just might destroy us all.

The Word for War

Japanese farmers rise early to work in their fields.
A few, eyes bleary with sleep, see the light
flash up and out. They do not know the source of it,
nor have they heard the roar of the bomb.
Light travels faster than sound; sound travels faster
than the wind pushing behind it; and death
doesn't bother to look up the word for its business.

For William Heyen

This Morning

the rains start to clear
in the west, and as the sun
begins to rise, it is in the west
that the light first appears.
Back to the east, the sky
remains dark while the rain
continues to fall, as if the earth
had changed its mind, turned
and walked the other way.

Somewhere Else

Your house sank down toward the swamps
south of Bulldog Crossing, trains hollering
each night on the other side of the water, light
trailing across duckweed, lily pads, the bass
who swam in and out of the rotten trunk of an elm.
By fourth grade you were drinking Pabst
on the front porch. Father gone most of the month
with Conrail, his days and nights shuttled back
and forth between Chicago and St. Louis,
and your mother too drunk to care much about
her oldest boy taking to her ways: smoking
Lucky Strikes and cursing Jesus, hitting
the other kids who sat fixed before the blue glow
of the TV. I can't even say you were different
after the Accra Pac Plant blew—neighbor burnt
so bad they bandaged him head to foot, you calling
him Mummy, making fun of his mumble, the fact
he had to have seven surgeries to get his lips back.
No, long before that you told me this was all there was:
we could play football in high school, we could get high
and take our place in line at the factory. We did play:
you were noseguard; I was tackle. You were drunk
half the practices, but come game time you were more
than sober, hyped on speed, somehow determined to show
everybody that if life was fair, you'd kick it through
the uprights, live over on Greenleaf Boulevard
like the pricks who owned the factories, drove
their Cadillacs like it was something religious.

You said if you had what they had, you'd be fishing
most days from a pontoon, red and green lights
reflected in the St. Joe, instead of sitting here
in the dark. Cane pole propped in a cement block,
bass not biting, a 48 ounce open and half drained,
broken glass sticking up in the gravel that slopes away
from the railroad where last January you stepped
in front of the train that runs less frequently
these days, goddamn trucks carrying more
and more of the weight to somewhere else.

First Snow, after September 11th

Last night the wind came strong
from the north, brought black
walnut and maple limbs back
to earth—fence row cluttered
in despair. Across the field
a crow beats his wings
against heavy clouds.

Can We Remember?

As I walk in this field, the last asters crumble,
their purple turned black by a hard frost.
The long heads of prairie grasses break
in my hands, plucked, then tossed skyward,
only to settle back into a life that will begin
in earnest come spring. In the middle of all this
I think of war, how inevitable it seems to most,
like this crow who flies among other crows,
circles over a distant stand of pine, then lands.

The towers have fallen. All that is left sits
in a hole: dust of bone, twisted flesh of steel,
the furtive movements of its apparitions.
Are our protests like these ghosts, like
the awkward voices of the crows
that accompany them?

Heavy machinery clears the pit, makes way
for more machinery. Wheels turn, metal clanks,
the earth shudders: today there is the threat of war.
There are also these asters and the dying grasses
that lie down in strong winds. Can we remember
what has fallen? Can we help what will grow?

For Yorifumi Yaguchi

A Country Lost

The boy and his brother have taken
their guns and gone to the woods
to kill crows as their father has asked.
They are good at this task, believing
with their father's fervor that the corn
must be saved. To the left of the older
boy, a large bird flaps up and away,
but not before he can bring the rifle
to his shoulder, sight-line drawn,
trigger squeezed with ease, motion
so fluid you'd think it was not learned.
The bird falls less gracefully to the ground,
and when the boys get to its side they see
it is an owl. The one whose rifle is still
warm knows they must bury the bird;
no one can find out about this death.
But its yellow eyes will not shut,
and the white feathers on each side
of its head and underneath the beak
stand out cleanly from the rest
of its dark body. That night in his bed
the boy dreams of shovels and hands
covered with dirt and blood, of wings
that begin to flap again and feathers
that fall like hard rains, like fists
upon his back, like a father who turns
away from a country he has lost.

The Bell

A farmer walks the slope just below
the edge of the field where it is too steep
and too rocky to plant. In the evenings

with the first snows of winter, he comes
to the green of old hemlocks, waxen cloak
of rhododendron grown taller than any man

in town. News of war travels across
the country: atrocities chronicled in numbers
that soon become meaningless, in photos

of the dead, some beheaded by the broadsword,
others blown beyond recognition by bombs, even
more made blind or dismembered by the technology

of our hatred. Under branches snow filters
down like the dust that settles after air raids.
The farmer listens to the town's bell, its cry

carried beyond the houses that sit miles away.
He knows he must cross two rivers to get
to that place. In his woods, as in town,

the hour grows late.

Learning to Speak the Words

When I write and you speak
the word *dirt,* may we feel
our tongues roll over
its coarse grains, black taste
of humus. And when the word
for *water* begins to drip
from the cave of our mouths,
may our bodies be buoyed
by the knowledge of it.
And of *air,* may our mouths
open to its aspirants, our lungs
full, lips unfurling like sails.
May we remember not to say
sun until we are ready
for the seed, planted in us
from the beginning, to take
root in our bellies, tickle
our throats, thrust from
our mouths—a vine climbing
toward the heat, so insistent
we grow.

The Movement of Deer

We come out of the woods, and deer spring
from where the meadow dips to the creek.
My uncle grabs my arm. Deer run

around us, current parted by our presence.
My father holds my mother, her face
sharp with panic. My sister stands

motionless in the moment. The herd's
movement lasts only seconds
before the final white flag flaps

up and over the crest of the hill,
and we are left alone on this dock—a sea
of tall grasses moving back and forth,

flashes of light farther out.

For Melinda Davis Lanham

Sitting High Up

on the tractor, the field looks more uniform
than it is, and it's hard to tell what causes
its surface to undulate, to swell like a brown

river whose current can shift and drag
the unsuspecting under, lost beneath rustling
cornstalks. At the end of August heat billows

like a dress on a clothesline, rises up, offering
a glimpse of what rests beneath, then falls back
toward the ground, as if nothing really happened.

Yet it has happened before and will happen
again—the fawn lying motionless, combine's blade
blind to what lines the field's floor, deer's right

hind leg severed as cleanly as a sawn tree limb,
and now this circle of red, like a tired sun, settling
back into the blackest soil.

Landscape with Dead Child

This is a poem about the old round and round with death.
How it stands before us doing a little boy's dance, black

leotard draped over bones, skull cap with holes as deep
as the wells we were warned not to lean over as children.

In this story, a boy digs in the mounds of dirt construction
crews pile when they build new homes. He makes holes

and tunnels, pretends they lead to the other side of the earth,
to the places in Africa and Asia his teacher tells stories about.

He doesn't know that death can't be held back by dirt,
that the boy who dances before him isn't wearing a costume.

Halfway to that other place, on this warm afternoon in September,
the sky falls, and when they finally find him, dig him out

from the black earth that holds his chest and arms, it's their eyes
that notice the arched backs of sycamore trees, the heavy heads

of goldenrod not yet cleared by frost, the last light of day turned
on its side, and the final lines of the same old story in which beauty

never brought anyone back from the dead.

Prayer Requests at a Mennonite Church

Pray for the Smucker family. Their son Nathaniel's coat and shirt were caught in the gears while grinding grain. Nothing would give, so now he is gone. We made his clothes too well. Perhaps this is our sin.

Pray for the Birky family. Their son Jacob fell to his death in the granary. He was covered in corn before they could stop the pouring—chest crushed by the weight, seed spilling from his mouth. We hope something will grow from this, besides our grief.

Pray for the Hartzler family. Their youngest has left the church and no longer believes that Christ died for her sins. She buys clothes at the mall. Tongue pierced, nose as well. Her shirt shows her belly where a ring of gold sprouts. We pray she will remember that her Lord's side was pierced, that His crown held no gold, only the dried blood of His brow.

Pray for the Miller family. Last week their daughter, who lives in Kalona, lost her baby at birth. Child only half-formed: head turned the wrong way; heart laid on the outside of her chest; one leg little more than an afterthought. Lord, help them know that life may come again, that we are all made whole in heaven.

Pray for the Stutzman family. Their son fights in the war. We call him back to the Prince of Peace, to our Savior who knelt to gather the slave's ear, brushed the dirt away, lifted it to the side of his flushed face. May we leave no scars. May we ask no blessing for the killing done in His name.

Trying to Understand the Patriot Act

Where I've been pulling stone from the edge
of the field, a mother killdeer screams at me.
She tries desperately to get my attention, pretends

her right wing is broken, letting it flop like a flag
at half-mast. Her nest must be near, but I don't see it,
nor hear the young she seeks to protect. When I come

too close to turn over a stone, judge its weight,
decide whether I can lift it into the bed of the truck,
she flies hard, up and away, banking, then drawing

a perfect circle across the field, showing me
the shape of air in the presence of fear.

Illusion

We've been burning prairie
grasses along the highway
today, offering the illusion
of control, as if the moving
arms of fire could be
choreographed.

Serviceberry

In my grandfather's time, before backhoes
and front-end loaders, the blossoms
on these trees spoke of an end to soil

hard as stone: all those who died inside
the white bed of winter stacked in coffins,
stored in sheds and barns, until mud once again

made its way back into houses on the bottoms
of boots, telling us that those we lived with,
and outlived, finally could be set in the ground—

a service for the dead draped in wreaths
the women made from these ivory blossoms
whose berries would not ripen until June.

Sleep

On the ridge above Skelp Road
bear binge on blackberries and apples,
even grapes, knocking down
the Petersens' arbor to satisfy the sweet
hunger that consumes them. Just like us
they know the day must come when
the heart slows, when to take one
more step would mean the end of things
as they should be. Sleep is a drug;
dreams its succor. How better to drift
toward another world but with leaves
falling, their warmth draping us,
our stomachs full and fat with summer?

Propellers

The farther west we travel
the prairie lies down
on its side to sleep.
Someone has left open
a window in this empty
house in the middle
of the country, and wind
blows through it day
and night. Like the maple
seeds we played with
as children, tossing them
toward the branches
they fell from to see
their green helicopters fly,
these wind turbines dot
the horizon, their long
metal blades flashing
in the spring sun,
their propellers pushing us
through the universe.

A Lesson in Mercy from My Wife, on the Last Day of May

A ladybug navigates the hair
on my chest; then, when it
reaches the skin of my shoulder,
she gently takes it between
thumb and forefinger, releases it
into the air where its wings beat
faster than the eye can follow,
where the brightness of the sun
makes it impossible to see.

The Name for Things

Because we call this purple
flower wild geranium
and that scarlet and yellow one
crown columbine; because
I have been taught this
hairy blossom belongs
to Virginia waterleaf
and that green umbrella
to the May apple—
whose fruit when fully
ripe is sweet, although
the seed at its center still
holds the consequence
of sin; because these names
are a catechism, this field
a holy book, all morning
I sit at the foot
of a Jack-in-the-pulpit,
grace of shade falling
upon me, sound of new
leaves and flowers tugged
by the sun's sermon,
the wind's hymn.

2

Learning to Read

Before seatbelt laws and airbags began to pull
families apart, you let me ride up front, seated
between your legs. My joy when you told me
I was steering, too young to realize you held
the wheel below, was incommensurate with the act.
But what more does a five-year-old wish for?

On the back roads of Michigan, signs sprouted
like goldenrod and Queen Anne's lace, and you
demanded I read them, pretending not to know
what to do if I didn't. The weight of your words
was nothing like the impress of the declarations
written in bold black on yellow, or the infinite space
white made when placed on a metal so red
children at slumber parties would tell stories
of the dead whose blood colored it.

No, this weight I carried came from the letters
whose meaning I worked hard to explicate, trying
to understand how they offered either absolution
or extinction—our very future depending upon
how I sounded out S-T-O-P. Knowing now
you would have stopped whether I could read
the sign or not, I understand that learning to read,
like so much of life, is about faith and doubt—
the possibility of one, the heaviness of the other.

At Six I Dream of Dinner with Neil Armstrong

I.

Standing on my father's chair, I help
my mother make Jell-O, peel tin
from TV dinners, stir Tang, pretend
to float free of earth's gravity, our house
and kitchen receding as my rocket
leaves the blue-green light
of the atmosphere.

II.

White and silver flecked formica encloses us
as my sister and I clean the kitchen after dinner.
Our first dishwasher shines with the promise
of some unknowable future, rests in the crater
between us, its hose connected to the sink
like an astronaut's tether.

At Buttermilk Falls

Water crosses these hills—snow-melt
followed by hard rain, the water that runs

out of the ground even in the coldest weather.
Water joins other water as it descends, makes

sound as it moves over rock and dirt, over
the bones of trees toppled in strong winds.

Water talks loudest when it leaps from
high places, hollows out the earth beneath it.

Near the falls the boy must lean close to be heard,
the reason his father brings him to this place.

How to Say Grace

When I was a boy, we danced in the kitchen
to Perry Como and Frank Sinatra, and my last

visit home, you danced with my son, his small
body curled into yours. Like your mother,

you prepare rutabagas and parsnips, potatoes
peeled and mashed by hand, a roast with carrots,

fried chicken, too. When we are full—cherry pie
and apple cobbler, ice cream perched upon it—

you tell us we need to eat more, hoping food
will save us, keep us until our next meal.

Snow Angels

We are all orphans:
whether our parents
die before our own
deaths, or simply vanish
like the snow angels
we made in the front yard,
the way they melted
when the first cold
rain of the year
fell: January thaw
thick with low hanging
clouds, banks
of fog
where wings
disappeared, feather
by feather, so many
fallen angels
released back
into the gray sky,
suspended
from the heavens,
wishing they could
stay with us,
like a blessing
to be
endured.

Ten Years Old, at My Grandparents' House

As we fall into sleep, stars descend,
attach themselves to lightening rods
and weathervanes, to the rooftops
of houses all across the valley—
their light not bright enough
to wake us, only warm enough
to hold us through this night.

Father's Hands

A little after three this morning, my father coughs.
Not able to fall back to sleep, he slides his hand
over the dimpled milk-glass of my mother's bottom.
She stirs, mumbles, pushes him away. In the kitchen
he drinks water, chews antacid, reads yesterday's paper.
Outside it has stopped snowing. Eight deer nuzzle
windfalls beneath apple trees. Between clouds
the moon shines, light sifts down like the flour
that floats in the air when mother makes bread.

Two doors from my parents' room, I drowse
next to my wife, naked and spent. The box
springs creak with the weight of each turn.
Her hands move through my hair, the way
my father's hands used to brush against
my cheek—a small boy sitting in the kitchen
after dinner, waiting for his weekly haircut,
then the sound of scissors near and brown
hair falling to the floor where soon mother
would sweep it all away.

Rules of Diplomacy

In a field to the west
of our home, two crows
chase one another.
The smaller of the two
holds something white
in his beak—piece of paper,
scrap of bread found
in the trash. The larger
hectors with wing-beat
and craw-cry, then dives,
forcing his companion,
his enemy, toward the earth.
Long before any true
collision can occur,
the smaller lets loose
the white, and it floats,
flutters like a broken wing,
lands undisturbed
in pasture. The two
birds swoop away
over the tree line.
Neither returns to claim
what each thought
was so precious.

Buck Day

Technicolor ghosts draped
in safety orange slide from
behind trees, drag the dead
down hillsides, leave red
trails in the snow.

What the Woodchuck Knows

The woodchuck knows not to stand down wind
from his own hole, that lawn tractors and combines
are far more dangerous than dogs and coyotes, that the morning
sun crests the tallest sycamores at the meadow's eastern edge,
reveals the ripest pawpaws that grow along the river's bank.

The woodchuck also knows that pear blossoms do not
keep late ice storms at bay, that the dew in the tall grasses
washes as well as the rain, that the den dug today
will be the fox's in the season to come, and that when
blind pups nurse, eyes should open to other things.

The woodchuck knows that the best meals make the worst
smells, that while sleeping beneath the earth, one can hear
the movements of the world above, can dream about the snows
that will fall in early December when sleep and dense clouds
muffle the footsteps of the few who foolishly stay.

In the end, the woodchuck knows what he needs to know:
that the North Star shines every night—whether cloud
or clear—and that each evening we should lift our heads
to see what we can see. Teeth last only so long
and life ends soon thereafter.

The Certainty of Weight

The winter after my father fell from a ladder
trimming the ash tree in the front yard, the snow

came heavy. By the end of December, our roof
began to creak, its load more than four feet deep.

In January, I climbed the peak of our modest Cape,
shovel in hand, tossed snow outward, watched it fall

carelessly to the ground—so much weight hurrying
through the air, only to stop with a certainty

that helped me understand how my father's spine
had come apart, how after so much effort

he had stopped moving, silent as he waited
for someone to find him.

Yet Another Life

What else could you do
having been ridden by love
for so long? We should have

expected you to rise up
on hind legs, to kick the stall's
gate in grief, spit out the bit

and bound recklessly into lust's
illusory race. Even so, it hurt
to see one who had run so well

stumbling—as if he wished
for the bullet, an end to what
was broken. Legs no longer

able to carry the weight; stone
laid heavy over her with no
hope for a return to things

.as they should have been.
Despite this, the hand held
back, gun again upon the rack.

Today we see you near the river,
tall grass soft on belly, water
cool against flanks, your head

moving up and down to counter
flies. The recognition that scars
bear more than flesh uncut.

For Donald Hall

A Sonnet for My Father, Just Before Dark

After I wash the Sunday dishes, the house is quiet, save
for the sound of leaves falling slowly through the air.
Like monarch butterflies, the reds and yellows of maple
and ash have yet to lose their color, and with the wind
that comes out of the west, they do not so much blow
along the ground as shuffle like an old man who no longer
aims for anything in life and is the happier for it. On the table
beneath the bay window, October light enters the room
like a hand holding a peach, and where my mother sits
in her chair, mouth half open, eyes closed, sleep's long
branches brace her body. On the stone path that leads
to the barn, the aimless old man raises his arms to the sky,
stretches, then kicks the leaves on toward the meadow,
where he will see what else he might do before dark.

Field Dressed

Because the doe wears neither seams
nor buttons, she will not come undone
easily, clothes falling to the floor
in a heap. If the meat is to be saved,

my knife must do its work: blade lifted
towards the fullness of breastbone,
intestines and stomach carefully pushed
aside. Her coat parts beneath the pressure

of whetted steel, wind-pipe and esophagus
cut and tied like a scarf; then the muscle
between her hind legs, the skirt of pelvic
bone, anus knotted so as not to ruin the dress

where my hands are lost in the pockets
of flesh, where now my fingers work loose
what was folded and packed so neatly
into the cavity of her chest. I hang the rest

of her like so much laundry on the line—
wet shine of blood dripping to the ground,
meat cooling, her life lifted, and my own heart
ragged, beating against what I've done.

For Rick Bass

Hunger

The closer we get to the top of the world
the more precise language becomes.

Hands move across ivory, carve the runners
of meat-sleds and the knives that will cut

the meat those sleds carry. In a place
where snow and cold kill without favor,

a word must be like a sharpened blade,
the hot tip of iron whose scar stands for

only one thing. These people ask for
the lives of animals to sustain them,

to buoy the bulk of their living,
and such questions cannot be tainted

by ambiguity. It is with clarity that a hunter
stands above an air-hole, spear ready

to strike downward through the top
of a seal's skull. How can any of us say

no to the question oxygen asks, to the hunger
of those who wait patiently, breath escaping

in white clouds, as they practice over and over
the word that means *enough?*

How Else

would God enter this room except through curtains
of light, muslin sliding over your hip as you lie
on your side? And what of the leaves beyond

the window pane that turn first to the sun, then back,
as if invisible hands held the course each must take?
What more evidence might we wish for to believe

that certain spirits travel from east to west? Surely
this late moon that hangs against the color of the coming
day, a blue that will fade before noon, holds everything

we will never understand.

Billy Sunday Considers the Second Coming

Most summer mornings in the fields
to the east of the house, hundreds
of spiders lift their webs to the early light—
fragile, tenuous, like a ball hit down
the third-base line just beyond the glove's
reach, a strand of silk undulating beneath
the blue and our team down two runs.

Loss becomes a sure thing, the stands
empty, and only the few faithful come
to watch this long, rocky patch brought
on by doubt, all of us dangling like a spider
over a flame. Nothing the manager says
makes any difference, and no one's sure
who to blame. My father used to say
that losing is like being lost—you keep
going through the motions, walking
from place to place, but you don't
recognize anything, especially not
the pitch you should swing at.

Still our wives keep telling us to believe,
that the only way to get out of the fire
is to climb back up the web. It hasn't
happened yet, but maybe next May
when the grass is as green as it'll get,
and the infield is raked smooth as wheat.
On that day I bet we'll hear the crack
of a bat, ball skidding in the dirt, see
the throw from right field sailing back
toward home plate, and all of us, because
we kept believing all along, running for
home, Jesus with his cap in hand
waving us in.

Litany

We assure each other the days must grow short.
        Yet our lamentations over the darkness that binds us
                to this season are like the grouse's cry, useless

in its petition for the sun to return, to rise on wings
        and roam freely above our heads. And so on this
                Thursday in January, cold rain seeping from the sky,

ground closed and water running off
        with the river, we know no language can hurry
                the light from its perch. Like the litany the minister asks

us to speak each Sunday in church,
        words will not make God walk across the earth
                any faster, heat of the sun flying at his back.

The Beginning of the Story

In the movie that the teacher shows our fourth-grade class, the small
Indian boy goes into the forest in the fall of the year to select a piece of
wood—perhaps the limb of a cedar, its green smell bringing the rotting
leaves that line the floor alive. He carries it to his home high in the
mountains where he sits before a fire, carves lines in the wood until the
frame of a man emerges—paddle fixed upon his lap as he waits for the
currents to pull his canoe toward open water. The camera catches the
boy's prominent nose, reminds me of the commercial that runs each
afternoon between Bugs Bunny and Daffy Duck cartoons: Indian Chief
standing near a garbage dump, a tear rolling down the creased skin of
his cheek. In the movie, snow falls with a silence that seems safe, a
heaven for Mohican or Anishnabe. Then the next frame brings
spring—first day when water drips from the roof, reflected sunlight
caught like dust in the projector's beam. Rivulets form in snow, gray
boulders take shape, and the boy again walks into the forest where
beneath hemlock boughs he places his boat. The best part of the
movie now begins for the rest of the kids. The canoe washes down
the mountain into rivers below, makes its way to a city harbor enclosed
by buildings so tall that they cast shadows over the water that stretches
outward, as if it has no end. When the lights come up in our
classroom, fluorescence upon varnished hardwood floors, I wish for
the movie's mountains, to run after deer with the Indian boy, a friend
I will never betray, both of us happy to be nowhere near a city or its
dumps, nowhere near a sea, instead always somewhere near the
beginning of the story.

3

What Comes Next

There was blood—the darkness of it, the burnt red
of wild blueberry in October. It ran from between
her legs, across the broad white flesh of her thighs.
With our first son the skin thinned but not enough

to keep her from tearing. That summer we grew
sunflowers, their heads round, so large that a storm
in August lashed them to the ground, twisted their stalks
but did not kill them. The birds came to feed on their faces,

offering some kind of reason for their misshapen lives.
When our second son's shoulders hooked against her insides
and they cut her in a vertical line, I worried the blood
that bathed the openness, that washed round his neck,

would drown them both. Instead his clavicle gave way,
easy snap of dead wood. They made me bathe him
while they sewed her back together, neat as a baby's
blanket and just as white. What if she had died?

What if the river I saw washing away beneath her
had carried her into a night with no moon?
Surely I would have stumbled, tumbled headfirst
over rocks, fallen trees. Prayer would have been

the only possibility: Asking for the moon,
for some kind of light to aid my search, for a path
to the river where I would wash the brown tracks
of dried blood from her body. And yet another prayer:

For the sun to rise, for her to squint, holding a hand
to the sky, shading the brightness from her face,
her smile as she sees me standing over her, my own face
open to what comes next.

While We Wait for Spring

The last three days snow has fallen.
No thaw this year, no day even above
twenty since the end of December.
Climbing the hill, my two boys slip, fall,
stand again. They complain, but there's nothing
to be done except to make it to the top
where above the trees we will look down
upon the river. Near the peak a barred owl
releases from the limb of a burr oak, sweeps
over our heads and out above the tree line.
Our eyes follow its flight to the river ice,
current moving beneath its blue surface.
Like the owl, our breath rises, drifts
toward something warmer, something better.

Forest Noir

A fisher takes up in the hemlocks south of our hay field,
begins the con with innocent strolls near the stream, eating
berries and beechnuts, not letting on that later there are those
he will stalk and kill. For weeks I find no sign of him, except

for his scat, full of seeds and not much more. But today
while walking, new snow on the ground, I stumble upon
a porcupine, rolled onto his back, throat torn and ruffled
like a red-tipped carnation. I can't help but think about

E.G. Robinson, duped and dragged into the nasty business
of death. Small man draped in an overcoat of quills, shifty
eyes moving from side to side, scared he might be fleeced,
yet unable to stop himself—the allure of the shadows,

the possibility that Ann Sothern needs him as much
as he thinks he needs her. In the black and white of winter
night falls with a deftness that makes temptation too much.
After weeks of clouds, who could resist a dress split up the side,

leg lifted to reveal the stocking's snapped garter, purple teats
of a porcupine laid bare in nice neat rows? Beneath the boughs
their story is written in their tracks: How the fisher waited
on the trunk of a fallen tree, how the porcupine tried to waddle

to safety but couldn't avoid the claws of his tormenter—
blow after blow to the head, until E.G. wept for the wife
he'd left, lifted his head to the heavens, resigned to the fact
he had done wrong: Ann Sothern was never his in the first place,

and these streets were far too far from home. In the end
the fisher sunk his canines into the pink that rests beneath
the skull, left his victim with nothing more than a final thought—
the realization his trail would lead back to his den, to the only animal

he ever truly loved.

First Step

In the picture my sister sent me
from the town's paper, an albino

deer lowers its head to the water
that floods the field. Rain has fallen

all summer in Wisconsin, and the river
has spent most of June and July

out of its banks. The water covers all
but the rotting tips of soy beans, bears up

a second deer, as white as the first.
Beneath the darkening sky

these twin moons float, until one
takes a step and the other flounders.

Jacklighting

In this part of Pennsylvania, roads run along
streambeds, or beside the narrow tributaries
the highest ridges conceal when they turn
their faces to the north or south—creases

marked the length of their long necks, ravines
as beautiful as the shadowed space at the base
of a woman's throat. In these little-traveled
places, the men who have been without work

for weeks and weeks take their trucks out
into the dark to find deer, to capture them
in the gaze of their highbeams, so they might
kill, come back to their homes with more

than the defeated faces they wear as they pay
for milk and bread with food stamps, their few
real dollars laid down for a pack of Camels
they'll smoke as they gut the animal in the barn,

taking what they can, dumping the rest along
the river where winter snows bury the arcs
of the deer's slender white ribs.

After Andrew Wyeth's "Jacklight" (1980)

That Kind of Death

A coyote slinks along the edge
of the field, stops to listen, to look
behind him, like a nervous boy
beaten by his father when the man
comes home from work, fists
balled in anger, an answer of sorts
to the questions the rest of life asks.
The sun is at the horizon, its light
orange and purple like a bruise.
The canine's coat glistens, his jaws
red with that kind of death
his father has taught him
so much about.

Communion

On this Sunday morning
a red-tailed hawk perches
on a hay bale in the middle
of our field, bows his head
and tears sweet flesh
from the chest
of a mouse.

Saint Francis Preaches to the Birds

Hundreds of fox sparrows roost
in the crowns of red and white oak.

Running the hill away from our house,
I stir them and they roll into the sky,

drawing a veil across the midday sun.
When we look up, all that's left

is broken blue pottery laid end to end,
a mosaic that tells the same story

I've been reading to my sons:
Saint Francis preaches to the birds,

speaks about the lives of animals,
their souls like leaves flaming

with the first frost, colors fading
to dust, joining the earth, so our feet,

when bare, might tread this path
to heaven.

Moonrise Over the Little Juniata

Skelp Mountain holds the roundness of light
as it rises in the east. The ridge hides most
of the moon well into the evening, while in the valley,
where it's still dark, we can see the silhouette of shale
and sandstone, delicate appendages of trees
along the top of the crest. The moon's body
in June is soft, supple, forgiving. When it finally
begins to lift itself above the edges of the horizon,
the breezes that run along the tops of the mountain
buoy it, help it float across the inlet of the sky.
On the surface of the river, it bobs with the moving
current, washes on toward Huntingdon on the chest
of the Little Juniata, always returning to the place
it started: water over rock, moon over water, rock
lost beneath the craters of the risen moon.

For Jack Troy

A Father's Notes

I must remember, now you are nearly eight
and your brother five, that my anger passes
to you so easily, climbs the river's bank
and floods the field, drags part of the earth

back with it, then carries us far away
from each other. And when I come into
your room in the early hours of the new day,
I should listen to your breathing, touch the back

of your head, follow the pattern your hair
makes, light strands at the side of your face,
my mouth close to your ear asking forgiveness
for the ways I fail you, predictable as my own

father's failures. And all of this will lead
to those times when you look across a field
where no one has stepped since the snow stopped
falling. In this place do not forget there are paths

we cannot see, that while no animal's track
marks the river, there is still direction
without its print. Consider the wind, busy
all night as it moved from tree to tree—

it offers one way, the snow another.
Whichever you choose, know I will follow.

First Day of School

I envy your ability to
See these things: the blind hands
Of the aged combing the sunlight
For pity

        —R.S. Thomas, "Because"

Today is my oldest son's first day of school after summer break—new grade, new school, new state. He doesn't seem too worried about all of the changes. But this morning I dream of a leper colony—although I haven't read about one for years, or even seen one in some late-night movie that gives us suffering so our hero can crash onto the set and save a lovely doctor, her full breasts peeking out from the sheer-white medical smock she wears to show her professionalism. No, in my dream a woman with dark skin—darker even than the center of a black-eyed Susan—holds her once-beautiful hands out to me across the surface of a stainless steel table, the kind my veterinarian father had in his exam room when I was a kid. We're enclosed in a cage with no roof, bars sunk into the ground like gray, rotting teeth. The earth spreads out from the cage—sand and rock—nothing green in sight. The sky falls away in blue and white patterns that reflect the local custom of drawing upon the skin of the sick in order to heal them. Because I can do nothing for this woman—I have no surgical tools to cut away the disease, nor any antiseptic to cleanse her wounds—I begin to pick pieces of red and black flesh from the floor, from the bars, from the shining table. I know this is a dream. I woke at 6:00 this morning, stumbled to the bathroom, and when I lay down again there were only a few minutes to sleep before the alarm. Yet I don't want to wake. For some reason I'm sure if I can find a way to help her, she'll tell me how to love my son better, how to make tomorrow and the next day less about pain and more about the way water feels when it closes around the body. Just as she begins to speak, the clock radio goes off, and on

The Writer's Almanac Garrison Keillor begins to recite a poem by R.S. Thomas. In hushed, Midwestern tones I hear about the world, the way it digests itself, thin flames scouring its face, how viruses invade the blood and flowers whither on the grave. With no hint of malice, Thomas writes that "this is what life is, and on it your eye sets tearless, and the dark is dear to you as the light." All I want is light for my son as he goes off to school today. But before I can send him out the door, he asks me about the fish we caught yesterday in the pond near the woods—a sunfish that swallowed the hook too deep, the struggle we had with the pliers, pushing and pulling, hoping that the metal barb might come loose. It finally did, and we released the fish back into the water. At first it tried to swim toward the bottom, as if healing might be found in darkness, sheltered in the depths below, as if the way water wraps every part of the body might close the wounds we'd made. But then it floated back to the top, wrinkling the sky reflected there, and began to swim in blue circles, flapping against the water's surface over and over, like a pair of hands clapping.

Adirondack Suite

I.   A raptor circles just above
Cascade, then down toward
where we sit on Pitch Off.
On this page I put my pack
beneath my head and lie
on a makeshift bed, watch
what is honest about
the hawk's flight: no guilt
here; nothing to conceal.

II.   Blue haze of berry shines black
with oil from our fingertips.
Huckleberries tie tongues—no talk
as we pick and eat, taking more
than an hour to fill our bucket.
How precious these berries become
to us who handle them only once
a year; how quickly they pass
from us, blue bushes grown green,
spreading along the mountain's border
as birds spill seed without care.

III.   Because it started to rain halfway
down the mountain, it begins to rain
between the words of this poem.
And because my son placed his right foot
on a rain-slicked rock, fell forward
more than ten feet, slid and skidded,
ending with a thud against unmoved
and unmoving gray granite, here he slams

his upper thigh into the sharp edges
of the words that speak of his pain:
purple *bruise,* red *scrape.*
But unlike that day mired in mud
when I yanked him by the arm, asked
if he was alright, fear and anger hung
together like tree limbs crossed
in a wind storm, I write this poem
to undo my own fall, to find a word
that will draw him to my chest.

IV.   Moosewood bows its leafy head,
        antlers shedding water upon our packs.
        The sun hasn't shown its face
        for five days: no blue above, no light
        to fall down the backs of leaves
        and land where ferns preen—only mud
        and standing rain, rivers rough
        with run-off. Still there is the blue
        of lily beads, the red of bunchberry
        and earliest hobblebush, even the pink
        of your face, wet with exertion.
        I'm glad you choose to walk
        ahead of me—your smell, strong
        as garlic cloves and sweet onion.
        When we stop for water, I wipe sweat
        from your cheek. When you turn
        and begin again up the trail, I bring
        fingers to mouth.

V.   Halfway up Tupper—no skiing
the last two years now the mountain
is for sale—a bear beds down
after beating his way through berries:
feast interrupted by blues and blacks,
deepest red on a changed horizon.
Sleep for a time and a dream of suckling
milky teats, gray and pink and sweet
as honey, then wakefulness with yet
more hunger as he lumbers to the north,
leaves these broken canes, this trampled
grass where we lie, bodies dwarfed
by his, an imprint of the dark
we all wallow in.

For Helen Kiklevich

How Like the Life

This morning around 2:30 Nathan crawls
into bed between us, comes into the warm
cave of our bodies—your breasts, my belly.
How like the life we hoped for this is:
moon, full last night, sits at the western edge
of the sky, languid like water that pools
near a bank in the stream, hemlock boughs
draped downward over the face of our child
whose sleepy hands rise and fall as they rest
upon the soft swells of your chest, wind blowing
gently on the crest of the next hill, high up
in the branches of an elm.

The Doe

October's light grows more distant
as I run along the path where the mulberry's
still-green leaves have let loose, catalpa and locust
leaves gone as well, seed-pods still strung
from branches like beans waiting for harvest.
Last week was warm, winds strong out of the south,
and the path was bare except for a scattering of black
walnut husks. On that day, near the river's bend,
I heard movement in the trees—just off the path
a doe not more than an arm's length away, shoulders
and belly already large with fat. She started, two steps
toward the river's bank, then realized nothing
could save her except some act of kindness.
My decision to continue had less to do with kindness
than the beating of my own heart, breath labored
from having come so close. This afternoon
as I run, I see the water moving through
the empty woods, and I wonder how many
names this river has had, how many trees
have grown large from its floods, like this basswood
that rises up over the tops of these other trees.
At the bend I can't help but think about the doe,
how that night she must have moved from woodlot
to woodlot, threat of hunters' guns forcing her
to make a way among the trunks of smaller trees,
their branches the gray of her winter coat, how
in fatigue she lay beneath the slow fall of ash
and hickory leaves, blessed by their yellows
and reds, by the all but forgotten brightness
of last summer's sun.

At the Fall Festival

The Amish man takes my oldest son's hands, places them
upon the crank, then walks back and forth between
two pine posts, strands of hemp strung out in his own
knotted hands. He attaches the twine twelve times
to two hooks on each post, gives his okay with circled
thumb and forefinger, and my boy begins to turn
the crank clockwise, each string part of another and then
another, until the twelve have become one, coarse
and warm, smell of friction in the air as the string constricts.
The Amish man takes the newly formed rope, tapes its ends
so his work will not unravel, then uses a gas torch to burn
the small bristles that hang from it like so much uncovered
hair, undone and useless. In the purple and orange light
of the torch's flame, he looks to my son, and without a smile
says that Jesus would have done well to have used a bit more
fire to keep his twelve from having come undone. And I wonder
when my boy will learn to fear God, as so many do—fire
and dread and love entwined in a tie that such rope binds
to our past and to the guilt that grows there like a vine.
Most of the ride home he is quiet, playing with the rope.
I am quiet, too, still hoping he doesn't understand.

Potatoes

We dig potatoes, dirt falling
away in clumps, voices
dropped, then picked up
again, rough surface
of our conversation, solid
at its center, as we place
full baskets in the cellar
for long gray days, cold
November rains.

Late in the Year

All that's left
along the river
is sumac, its horn
turned the same
color as the rust
the empty oil
drums wear.
The yellow
scarf of dying
grasses drapes
them both, weary
as the waters
whose weight
trout bear up,
their bodies
changed by
the ceaseless
movement
to which they
were born.

Shelter

Under the first blue sky
      in thirty-eight days, the ice
            thins. Geese rest their feet

upon its drifting edges, and out
      where the river grows wide
            and deep, a small island of trees

hides the animals who have made
      their way to it in the heavy cold—
            ice firm, snow swept from its surface,

a momentary bridge to fir and hemlock,
      boughs pushing against wind, holding
            these few through the winter and into

the long days of summer, until the snow
      falls again and again the river freezes
            and at last the way to the far shore opens.

12 Songs for a Long Winter

I.   In a field above the road
that leads out of our village,
a doe steps gingerly across
the white crust, snow devils
at play among broken corn stalks.
Every two or three steps she breaks
through, flounders like a drowning
man whose lost faith prevents him
from hearing the songs the waves sing
as he settles to the ocean's floor.

II.   Deep winter cold slides
over us. In the pine boughs
at the back of the house
crows roost. Come morning
the ground is littered with shit:
muddy-yellow, black against white.
Today the earth's mouth remains
closed, as it will every day
until spring, when in the warmth
it opens and swallows everything.

III.   Tonight a nor'easter moves
inland, sweeps over the mountains
with a magician's black cape.
Along the river's banks mink tunnel
in the deepest snow, circle within circle,
until they disappear, like the woman
from the audience who volunteers, steps
into the austere box, magician tapping it
three times, leaving nothing for our eyes
except the darkness of night filled

with the white silk handkerchiefs
of flying doves.

IV.   There will come a day in midsummer, somewhere
near the heat of the sun, when the air is as full
as a spilled cup, water seeping back to its source—
on that day, in spite of ourselves, we will wish
for the early dark of late December, snow falling,
dead leaves pulled across the entrance to our den.

V.   Wind continues to turn all day
while snow squats on mountains.
Here clouds consume everything,
like hungry giants who climb down
the great stalks of oak and ash
in search of lost children
only to find branch water
spun into stone.

VI.   In early January, after three days
of thaw, hard cold clings to the sun
as it climbs the far peak. My sons
laugh as they walk on top of the snow,
as confident as Peter's first steps
upon the sea. Even my wife and I
venture out, amazed to stand upon
white ridges, canoes and sailboats
shaped by thaw and freeze, until
my left foot falls, vanishes beneath
three feet of snow, a white ocean of fear
despite my children's calls to have faith.

VII.   This past fall the farmer down the road
       stacked round bales of hay in long procession.
       Like electrical wires strung together, white
       plastic draping them, they protrude, burnt out
       bulbs where there is little light until May
       when again the grasses begin to glow green.
       Amidst this wire and wattage, a young bear
       has bedded down in the cave of the farmer's
       making, torn the plastic so he can push hay
       across the entrance to his makeshift den.
       Because he is young and his mother
       was struck by a car in July, he has fallen
       behind in the autumn months, not enough fat
       to carry him upon the river of winter's sleep.
       Now, in the deep bed of snow, he treks out
       to feed every few days, his scat telling us
       what we already suspected—to eat in dream
       is to know hunger when we wake.

VIII. Part way through February, the roof of a barn
       gives out: rafters riven, floors fallen, burden
       of snow sending it all to the ground
       where it will begin to rot in the first warmth
       of April—fires of decay, sour smell
       of wet flames.

IX.   Ice jam groans in the middle of March, holds back
       its waters for the next few weeks. People downstream
       know it's only a matter of time before the river lets go,
       before the flood is sent into their streets and restaurants,
       their basements and living rooms. Upstream bets are made

about when the break will come. Town drunks show us
how to step from block to block, how to make our way
across the water's hard surface, sound of ice moving
so much like a woman's wailing.

X.   We watch the snow draw back
into the woods, like a tongue
into a mouth. Beneath the crest
of a granite outcropping, far up
in the hemlocks, a small swatch
of snow remains into early June,
reminder of an abscessed tooth
pulled last winter.

XI.   The river breaks up in the middle
of an April night, ice floating
downstream to melt in its journey
toward a warmer place. A raccoon
comes in the dark, pushes his feet
through water and sand, feels
for mussels, as relieved as a dish-
washer who scrubs his last plate
at the end of a long shift.

XII.   Almost May and still snow
is scattered in soiled banks.
Rain starts just after noon,
water washing over the river's
walls near the bend where cows

come to drink. A few days
from now, we will walk
the pasture, see what the river
has taken, what the winter
has left behind.

Pastoral, at the Start of the 21st Century

Black angus graze beside the stream,
its banks held back by fieldstone.
Where pasture ends south of the farm-
house, a tin building squats near

the highway—*Adult World* in pink neon
against sycamores and Indian willow,
against the Pennsylvania countryside.
Every day cattle come to drink

from the brown water that runs
east towards Huntingdon; every day
men back their cars into the gravel lot
so no one can see their license plates.

Like a bull entering a stanchion, each
man passes through the painted glass
to sit in a cramped booth and watch
women open themselves to other men.

And like the same bulls who are shown
heifers in heat and then must mount
the artificial cow made of worn leather
and cold rubber, these men catch their

seed in white tissue, all that they hoped for
already shrinking back into their hands
as the dark heads of cattle move along
the stream to the barn for the night.

Tattoo

Try telling the boy who's just had his girlfriend's name
cut into his arm that there's slippage between the signifier
and the signified. Or better yet explain to the girl
who watched in the mirror as the tattoo artist stitched
the word for her father's name (on earth as in heaven)
across her back that words aren't made of flesh and blood,
that they don't bite the skin. Language is the animal
we've trained to pick up the scent of meaning. It's why
when the boy hears his father yelling at the door
he sends the dog that he's kept hungry, that he's kicked,
then loved, to attack the man, to show him that every word
has a consequence, that language, when used right, hurts.

Spring Winds

The tall, straight trunks of cherry
speckle the mountainside, pale
blossoms like my son's smile
after a trip to the dentist, fluoride
protecting him from the youthful
nightmare of drills and syringes,
Novocain's numb promise wearing
off, leaving its victim with the memory
of fingers, the small justified violence
of care. Along the road, coltsfoot's
yellow flower has gone to seed, head
the same gray that creeps into my hair
now that a new decade has begun. In another
place, not as far off or long ago as we wish
to believe, dentists groped through dead
mouths for gold, guards fingered rectums,
vaginas, any fissure where jewelry or coins
might be caught up, away from the hands
of those who seized them, who sent them
staggering towards death's heat. How easy
it is to say that such people only live
in the past: soldiers and citizens gone mad,
possessed by a lunatic's promises, numb
to the larger violences they committed
with even greater care. I read these stories
when I was a boy, my father's collection
of histories shelved neatly on pine bookcases,
his need to understand the Germany
that existed little more than a decade
before he brought his new bride with him
to the Air Force base where he served
as veterinarian. And I was no different

than any other boy: the language of hell's
ovens, of lampshades made from flesh,
of showers spilling gas onto the floor
where the dead had already fallen.
The grotesque draws us into its maze,
makes us double back upon ourselves,
yet never asks us to imagine our own faces
drawn tight, dark hollows sunk in the caves
of our cheeks because we have not eaten
for days, our hair shorn for mattresses
and dolls, our hope slipping like a rope,
riding up over our necks a bit more each day.
Yet something other than this brings me back
to the warmth of the April I live in now,
and although when I began this poem I thought
I wished to write about the spring beauties
that overrun sections of the greening woods,
the lilacs whose fragrant hair falls across our fence,
the great rumps of skunk cabbage thrown
toward the heavens, I cannot forget the pallid
asses turned over, those who ransacked the flesh
of others, as if it were no more than a bag filled
with potatoes, as if their work was nothing
more than the search for the best tubers
to serve with the evening meal. There are those
who would like us to believe such times
have passed, like the forsythia's flowers, leaves
lifting, yellow petals dancing in the winds
that usher in spring. Yet we must bear witness
to the magnolia's blossom as it turns ashen,
droops, falls to the ground and begins to rot.

Once Again

Not long after the snows
are gone dandelions spring
up across the fields, green
only for a few weeks. In time
their heads turn white like old
women, hair blown by the wind
without any apparent purpose
or direction. Under the quiet
words of the warm sun, they nod
off in their pews, yet their seeds
fly gracefully just the same
and soon find purchase
on some patch of sod, growing
as if they knew all along
their flowers would once
again outshine the sun.

Ode to an Ophthalmologist

The doctor asks me to roll my eye toward the ceiling
so she can insert the small brace that will keep my lids
open during the procedure. For weeks the bump
has festered beneath my right eye—first a scab, then
ooze of pus, then another scab. The bright orange
antibiotic has not worked, nor the steroidal drops
that burned the eye, reduced the swelling, yet finally
could not conclude anything. Now this incision—
the only recourse to my sons' averted gaze, my wife's
pitying stare. Because I no longer look as intently
in the mirror as I did at fifteen—every girl a possible
dance partner, a potential kiss—I forget when others
see me that my eye droops, listless and lethargic.
I'm glad I feel nothing as the doctor scrapes clean
the wound she has made. She tells me the infection
looks like clear cottage cheese, reminds me to use
warm compresses, that the eye may still close shut
and again make a not so benign bump. What will
I take from this? A scar. The memory of the nurse
who became sick at the sight and had to leave.
How my eye opened again to the world; how it seemed
nothing had changed.

At The National Gallery Thinking of My Wife

Next to the tub you lean forward, arch your back
like the shadow of evening as it slides across

the sundial's face. The skin of your bottom blushes
with the blood warm water has brought to its surface,

and because at this hour our sons sleep in their rooms
you allow me as much time as I wish to watch you

prepare for bed. After carrying two babies into this world
your thighs and belly have blossomed. How glad I am to see

their fullness, to witness the garden at its most ripe; how I love
to follow the towel's line as it drapes your breasts, reveals

the muscle of your back, your arms unburdened
and the broad circle of your hips released.

After Edgar Degas's "After the Bath, Woman Drying Herself" (1888–92)

This Time Each Year

Toward the middle of May, redbud begin
to drop their blossoms, green entering
the room at the edge of the forest. Blood-
root, white flower gone in a matter of days,
throws its leaf over shoulders like a light
spring jacket. And lilacs wrap their arms
around each other, scent so strong
that as I ride my bike or cross the street
on foot, it billows up like clean sheets
taken from the line, shaken hard twice,
then gathered to the face. This is how
you steal into our room: hair soft on skin,
smell as familiar as your kiss, your flower
clinging to us as we awake.

Indiana Love Song

She cradles the basketball in her upturned hand—
limbs long, fingers relaxed. Love has led
her to practice this same motion thousands of times:
lift of elbow, single fluid push of wrist, rising

then curving down like the swan's neck as it
turns to feed. What else could a girl desire?
Her legs, waves that stretch to ferry her
across the free-throw lane where she accepts

the screen her teammate sets, an act of kindness
that asks nothing in return, save the knowledge
that for such gifts to be worth their giving, the one
who receives must cut close, rub shoulder to shoulder

so that the defender who trails can do nothing
to disrupt the single devotion this play requires.
And here she catches the pass thrown long
before she was open, the faith that timing

demands, the ball sailing across the lane
into her hands: right foot planted, heel first,
then shoulders squared, arms raised toward
the heavens, hidden by rafters where banners

hang—icons that cannot remember the mystery
nor the adoration the body possesses, always
called toward the basket to be blessed by the ball
that comes gently bending back through the hoop.

For Shelly Davis and Carol Owens

Beginning the Eighteenth Year of Marriage

Yes, our flesh sags a bit
where once we worked it
into tight fists, full
of the fury of love, and, yes,
around our eyes, wrinkles,
like leaves in September,
show signs of wear and want.
But even the threat
of frost can't quell desire's
turn: first fire of the season
built and burning, dark
smudge of soot on your breasts,
gray ash trailing across mine.

Some Heaven

The rabbit's head is caught
between the slats of the fence,
and in its struggle it has turned
so the hind legs nearly touch
the nose—neck broken, lungs failing.
My boys ask me to do something
but see no mercy in my plan.
At five and eight, they are so far
away from their own deaths
that they cannot imagine the blessing
a shovel might hold, the lesson
suffering offers those who have
not suffered.

At bedtime, my youngest prays
the rabbit is in a heaven
where there are no fences, where
there is more than enough to eat.
He begins to cry and we rock
until sleep's embrace takes him
from me. I know his prayer is right.
What more should heaven be?
A place wild with carrot and dill,
sunflower and phlox, fields
that stretch on for miles, every coyote
full, every hawk passing over, a warm
October day that need never end.

For Nathan Davis

Distraction

When we wake, our stone walls
are skimmed with snow, and all
through the woods the eastern sides
of branches and trunks are white
as well. In the meadow, the last bits
of green push up, then fall back
into November's waiting, yellow bed.
Along the edges, seven deer search
for food. Like early morning thoughts,
they browse lower limbs of maple
and sassafras, until the sound of foot-falls
coming from the dry creek sends them
into flight.

Enigma

And no one was able to answer . . .
Matthew 22:46

Early December. Most rivers covered in ice.
One blue heron still has not left. It flies up
and over the naked sumac, then lands—a thin, gray
question mark written on a sky that holds no answers.

4

Ars Poetica

Two native brook trout circle
each other, swim to the far end

of an eddy where oak and ash
have fallen, log across log,

so now the water falls five feet,
digs away sand, exposes a slab

of rock. It's the pressure
of moving water that gives

shape to this bed of gravel,
the place the spawn of these fish

must return to—never asking
what it means.

with deference to Archibald MacLeish

The Way Things Go

Ash and maple and hickory
leaves are falling into this poem
again, and again a deer walks
from beneath the trees into the open
space of the meadow my words
have made. Somewhere beyond
these margins five bear begin
their last meal—their path toward
winter's deep sleep as clear as the sky
that sits blue above this poem's first line.

Here fall chases summer, brings
down what we thought never could be
replaced. Winter clears it all away—
the page white until spring writes
upon it with green buds and purple
blossoms. How else would the light
get in, and where would we be
if we did not have the dark
to drift into? The earth carries us
upon her back. Where she turns
we should follow.

Catechism

We've been learning to pray
the prayer of the red eft, to make
the sign of the common egret,
to bend our heads in submission
in the presence of the animals
who give us life.

For Mary Linton

Annunciation

What is this weight of forgetting
we carry upon our backs?

Four below and all night winds bear
snow across the lake, drape every branch
with curtains that fall away from the sky's
open window, only to reveal the play of blue
with early sun, light laid down in turkey
and pheasant tracks. At the middle of this
shining, we walk into a basswood swale,
nothing to say we've been here, save our
footsteps, and they too disappear when winds
shift, and once again waters are gathered
to the sky, then released, like a hand opening
to sow seed that will cover this hill
in clover. Here everything we ever did
is lost beneath the drifts of our flesh, buried
until spring rains raise the streams
that run through June: waters washing
over bones gnawed open at their ends,
souls released by the teeth of porcupine
and field mice, the only bodies we've ever
known consumed, then shat out upon
the earth, where everything returns
to that other body made of dirt and water
and a winter's worth of manure, spread
on the field the first warm day of spring,
when trout lilies lift themselves near
the swamp and a thousand moons of trillium
illumine the forest's green floor.

For Jim Harrison and Dan Gerber

Canada Geese, on Saint Valentine's Day

Their calls woke me this morning, great wings
lifting and falling like bellows beneath a fire.
Two flocks flew over as my son and I walked
to the end of the road where each morning
the school bus takes him from us. The rest
of the morning the geese continued up
the flyway, talking to us about promises, about
the way warmth comes back into the ground,
how returning to a place you've loved
is one of the better things you can do.

Spelling Test

The mother makes the boy repeat the word aloud
three times, asks him to roll the sounds out upon
the edges of his tongue, the much talked of tip.
She tries to demonstrate the logic of the letters

following in a line, how each hugs the next
in friendship, fastens part of its own life to the life
of its neighbor: their voices in conversation, heads
bent out of windows, arms resting on top of fences.

Together they build something bold or something
shy, that despite their demeanor holds fast to meaning.
The boy's hands grow tired, clinched so tightly
white forms around the knuckles, until the word

has passed, until at last he lets go, sees language
can't be corralled. It's the lips after all—a smile,
teeth showing, tongue wet, and words slipping out
to taste every good thing we might remember.

For Noah Davis

Gravity

Tonight as I hugged you, muttered
the good-bye parents use to send
their children into the dark of sleep,
I felt the bump along your right
collarbone, calcium knit into a knot
where you fell one summer doing
cartwheels for a girl with brown hair.

This was the first lesson in love:
that gravity takes everything from us—
our balance as we wrestle the urge
to prove we are better than any
other, deserving love; or the lines
in our face, droop of ass, a slow
accretion we blame upon age
instead of acknowledging the force
that drags us into each other's arms
and always one step closer to the grave.

In Praise of Dürer's Dandelions

Although their yellow manes have yet to open, they hold
their heads high, regal as they rise from vellum, preen
and posture in painted strokes. By your hand's bidding
their leaves wait to be cut, then eaten, and in a few weeks
when their golden hair brims wine-making will commence:
press and crush of wood coming together with other wood,
juice leaking away into winter months when a bottle opens
and shows us the way back to this shining day. How wise
you were to note them—your age so different from our own.
But I note that ours is so different from all others and wonder
who was the first charlatan of the suburb to sell the dandelion-
digger, to name this most precious of plants weed? Observe us:
In this gallery we gaze upon your paintings, soft murmur
of appreciation so much like the sound of wind spreading
the dandelion's downy seeds, or the swish, swish of rubber
boots as men walk back and forth across our lawns, long hoses
held in gloved hands, lines running from white cylindered trucks
whose sides advertise in bold relief: death to everything
except the green, green grass.

After Albrecht Dürer's "The Great Piece of Turf" (1503)

Meditation on the South Skunk River

Walking the last of the river ice
we come upon a beaver, dead, only
its head lifted above the frost, body
lost beneath the water's white current,
posture set like a swimmer's, as if caught
mid-backstroke looking up at the stars
when the water began to freeze—life
captured not by cold or carelessness
but by the beauty that continues each day
to drift above our heads.

For Keith Fynaardt

Near the Center

Like the sky, the river is
frozen the blue of chicory
in midsummer. Out near
the center of the flow, beech
leaves hold still for the first time
since falling, framed in ice
so clear that our youngest
reaches for them only
to discover they do not
belong to him. I confess
often I reach for you
in this way, and at such
moments am reminded
that to watch the buds
build through February
is not a burden.

Her Time

The long steel teeth of the pitchfork
slid through solid white bone, flesh
and femur, when her foot slipped
from the two by four at the back
of the shed. She was my sister's
friend. Tall and gangly, her limbs
dangled like a pale praying mantis
or a marionette whose strings tangled
too often and too easily. Years later
I can't recall if she climbed to the loft
to kiss a boy, or to tell her girlfriends
what it was like to kiss a boy. I do know
she'd been warned of the danger—
how boys only wanted one thing, how
the shed held the tools that her father
and grandfather used to work the acreage.
Of course, none of this could stop her
heart from beating, slick blood pushing
up like a fountain from the pierced artery.
When a girl comes into her time,
nothing can staunch the sad beauty
of her bright red flower.

Nothing More

He was used to writing
poems during meetings
and student presentations,
voices droning like bees
when the azalea blooms,
or while driving his car,
trucks only inches away,
death in tow. As Graves
tells us, "To be poets
confers Death on us."
But death to self, or
to the world, or to each
moment passing away
irretrievably, irrevocably,
like the same azalea
days later, blossoms
black with decay?
What he liked most
was writing in church
while the minister
explained why Christ
said the child had
not died but only slept.
Poetry is nothing more
than lucid dreaming:
awake enough to change
the course of things
by merely desiring it,
asleep enough to know
the pleasures of the dead.
A poem can't say what
the girl wished for

after Christ called
to her, "Talitha kum."
But from what poem
would anyone willingly
awake? In the room
where Christ composed,
she slept undisturbed
until his words woke her
from a dream of mustard
grown taller than any
plant, of birds roosting
in its branches, shielded
from the day's harsh light.

Prodigal

After the second storm of the day, the sky is mostly
blue again. In the fields water collects in low spots,
rows of new corn push on toward the west
where white clouds hang their heads like sheep
held by children for shearing. Up and down
the county roads, Amish women walk barefoot
in their gardens, their pink and purple dresses bright
against the dark soil, peonies and Sweet William
clothed the same. A sign on State Road 19 tells
a son to come home, that Jesus still loves him
and God forgives, that the wages of sin is death.
To the back of Troyer's fence row, catalpa blossoms,
just opened yesterday, scatter upon the ground, prodigal
in their passing.

Just Before Milking

Hooves sunk deep in spring mud, cows dream
of leaves that will unfurl in coming weeks, brown
grasses resurrected by early rains, a sun that lingers
longer each day, beckons first to crocus, later to clover.
And in those fleeting moments before dawn, when all
their dreams seem most real, apple blossoms begin
to fall, a light breeze covering their tracks as they trail
down to the creekbed—barn left behind, pasture
all their own, a place where no rough hands
will wake them as they sleep.

For Ray Petersen

The Wash

Softest fingers of pink crawl
with the sun over the ever-darkening
greens of spring. Water slips through
the pasture like the blue line of a vein
strung down the back of a woman's leg,
never seen beneath her yellow dress
except when she stands on tip-toe
to hang the wash.

After N. C. Wyeth's "Autumn Brook (Late Spring Morning)" (1928)

When We Eat

the bread you bake, we should taste
the grain before it is crushed, give thanks
for the chaff cast out, look under our nails
at the dirt we carry with us, same as the field's
where now wheat climbs toward the memory
of late winter, clouds pulled under by the weight
of the first warm blue sky.

Foreclosure

Painted turtles sun themselves on a log
near the edge of the pond. Apple and pear
trees that haven't been pruned in more
than a decade fall across a broken fence.
Out buildings lean toward the east
like morning glories waiting for the sun
to break. The Yoder family no longer
leads the life of this place. Like turtles
who know when danger draws near,
they disappeared when the farms grew
large and larger still—ripples on the water's
surface spreading, rings of poverty
within rings of wealth.

Aftermath

In a room at the back
of the house, a tea kettle

whistles, voice rising
like the cry of a baby

unrocked in a cradle,
no song sung gently near

her ear. Steam slides along
walls, the ceiling, and a cup

filled with honey and lemon
waits on the counter.

Will no one leave this bed, go
and remove the flame, make

this cup, accept the blame?

Mid-May in a Year of Early Warmth

White cones of buckeye blossoms rest in the palm
   of the tree's five leaflets, resigned to the start of yet
      another spring, while the drooping white phalluses
         of black locust hang from twisted branches, indifferent

to the ridged bark of the tree's turning trunk. Strong scent
   of autumn olive wraps its legs around the back of this day,
      its small yellow buds as pungent as the all-too-sweet smell
         of a new mother's sickness—warm room late at night,

no breeze to ruffle curtains, to move the air that presses
   down upon her chest and swollen belly. Like her night gown,
      dame's rocket flourishes in ditches—four-petaled pinks
         and purples and whites on long green stalks that topple

when we walk into the fields already ripe for their first mowing.
   How we talk of ox-eyed daisies that spring up with no concern
      for what will come later; how in the midst of the February past
         we dreamt of choke-cherry, its bottle-brush cylinder of flowers

flung up like small fingers searching for a mother's breast.
   Did we really believe these blossoms that last a few short
      days could relieve us of the dying months, remove the dirt
         of the lives we live the rest of the year?

The Waters Are Rising Again

Rain the last five days, most of it slow
    and steady like an old woman walking
        up the street to the store where she buys

a loaf of bread, a quart of milk, gum and candy
    she gives to the children when they bring
        her paper and mail. Where the stream bends

its back around the western edge
    of Shipley's farm, water crests, starts up
        over the road that runs from Tipton to Bellwood.

This afternoon we hike the hill
    behind our house, follow the deer trail
        along the ridge, then down into a thicket

of mountain laurel and rhododendron—
    the only evidence of progress the sound
        the river makes as it drops over the largest stones.

We keep on until water stops us,
    so much earth washed away the bank juts
        out over nothing and soon will fall with the water's

rough song. Watching the river race on,
    we yell above the current, survey lawn chairs,
        tires, plastic tubs riding the tide, all the refuse we failed

to tie down before the storm, and the neighbor
    we've come to check on, waving at us from the far side,
        waiting for these waters to go back where they belong.

The Alewives

die by the thousands, pitching themselves
onto the shore, now warmth has come back

into the water. Against the sand their sides
no longer glisten. Their bodies rot in the sun.

This great lake shaped like water pouring
from a pitcher scatters them where park-service

employees haul them away with front-end loaders.
How the world has opened to these fish

who long ago swam from the Atlantic
to this inland sea. How quickly they perish

far from home.

The Trick

All morning turkey vultures
slide up the side of the ridge.
We sit beneath the firetower,
watch them appear
from the mountain's head,
like the magician who pushes
the pencil into his mouth
only to pull it from his ear.
We've seen the trick
more than thirty times
but still gasp at black wings
spread on thermal drafts, pink
head leering like an insolent
tongue, hooked beak, a pencil
pushed toward the eye.

Resurrection, or What He Told Me to Do When He Died

Take me to the field where the river runs
by the swamp. Dig a hole deep enough
that dogs and coyotes won't dine on
what's left. Place cedar boughs
beneath my head, cover my body with ash
from the fireplace, dirt from the garden.
Spread seed here and there in no particular
pattern. Don't visit until warmth comes back
into the earth and spring rains move on. Then
see how jewelweed sprouts from my chest
and clover climbs from my eyes.

Landscape

"She was just like blueberries to me."
—*Andrew Wyeth*

You walk from hill to hill, change
your vantage as the sun changes
its place in the sky, as a young woman
changes out of her clothes, stands
in her body before you.

In one place a buttonwood tree, spiked
seed strung along its limbs; in another,
a stream maned in mist. Later, making
your way back to the house, the land
becomes a woman asleep on the grass,
quart of berries picked and placed
at her side, precious fruit that will pass
in a matter of weeks.

On the Appalachian Trail, above Delaware Water Gap

Up on the ridge the October sun still sifts
down enough warmth that a few blueberry

come into second bloom. Early morning
and quiet. I've no reason not to stop, to sit.

The white bells of the blossoms look like souls,
auburn leaves like blood that must spill

if the soul is to depart. At this hour
the grasses wet my legs, spider webs

outlined by dew, by the blue above their nests.
In the distance two nuclear reactors send

steam into the air: ghosts of uranium,
plutonium, of water turned against itself.

Two hawks and four vultures have surfaced
while I've sat here. They ride the updrafts

that rise along the cliff face. They see a world
that will come long after these petals fall.

The Flowers and Their Fruits

The boy asks his father why
he works so hard to remember
the names of the field's flowers.
This desire for memory requires
the two walk each day into shades
of green that turn over and over
like children tumbling down
the hills of April and May
until they reach the bottom
of September's last days
when the first frost puts
an end to the blooming.
Despite himself, the boy
begins to rehearse the names:
foam flower and phlox, wild
raspberry and wood sorrel,
learns to recognize the tall stalks
of joe-pye weed and mullein,
the careful lace of yarrow
and wild carrot, and although
he shrugs when he is called
to walk, a bother to leave his play
with the neighbor boy behind,
in time he will come to understand
the only way back to his father's side
is in the memory of the names
of the flowers and their fruits.

For Wendell Berry

In the Middle of Iowa

they arrive, hundreds of pelicans
flying south for the winter, surreal
ghosts I never imagined outside
the tropical heat of Florida, my only
glimpse of them the vacation
to Disney World at twelve. Here
their wings beat in unison above
corn fields and combines. Here
they settle upon the shallow waters
of this lake like seaplanes at a resort.

Tomorrow the north wind will travel
down from Minnesota, from Canada,
from a place so white we would be lost
in the sun's glare upon its hard surface.
With this cold prophecy, these great birds
rise, bodies remembering the course
they must take: without lines or borders,
without a map of the known world—no
station wagon to carry them, no pink
and orange billboard to greet them, only
their souls connected by a thousand
other journeys they have made.

For Lucien Stryk

Wherever We've Traveled

After running along the road by the bay, we taste the salt
so essential to who we are: wherever we've traveled
it's been there beneath the crust of the earth, in the sea's
restless sleep when we've swum in the black pool
of summer's heat, streaking the sides of our bodies
when we kissed one another, the softer fruit of our flesh
broken open like the ocean when it swells and crashes,
swells and crashes.

Prairie Liturgy

Only upon our failing breath may we speak.

I.

Words are carried
like small boats on the river
of our blood, oxygen dying
in the sails, hands braced
on gunwales.

II.

Without trust, we hold the first
word, then the next and the next
after—a stolen prayer, an early
moon half-eaten, plum bruised
and laid upon the horizon's table.

III.

When will the hornet's nest, nestled
in the branches of the locust, begin
to flutter, its gray lung turned pink?

IV.

Fox and deer hide in the prairie's last
remnant, concealed by the ravines that fall
away like creases in the brain or the ridges

of a hedge apple, florid green and hard
as granite.

V.

What evidence of the bobcat? Only her kill—
tracks circled, hind paws leaping, a bird's
downy plume laid at the bottom of the creek
where water freezes come November and snow,
like a shroud, veils all until April.

VI.

A highway runs
where the ocean once lay,
and here winds blow for days,
birthed upon a sea, borne
up over mountains to the flat,
open space of this field.

VII.

The red-tailed hawk cares nothing
for judgment, sees no good or bad
as it sits on a mile-marker, waiting out
passing cars to dine on what we kill.

VIII.

We cannot hold
our breath
forever—in time
this prayer
will slip
from us.

IX.

Today the grasses rise and fall, as they do
at sea. And this bird's wing-beat helps
move the stems, takes the seed and delivers
it into the earth where the sun will drag it
toward heaven, all of our heads bowed
and bent by the wind.

X.

What else is there but supplication?
Bee dips into flower's bowl, bobcat's belly
full, small polished bones in the osprey's
nest, and scat of all kinds spread beneath
the basswood in honor of the lives taken.

XI.

On the plain that rises beyond the river,
September grasses begin to fire, smoke
visible for miles, great curtains of flame
opening and closing, telling a story
of a world without end.

XII.

Amen.

For Mary Swander

After Our Fight

In the field, snow hangs
from the brown heads
of goldenrod. On up
in the woods, I follow
the tracks of two deer:
stop to examine fresh scat,
urine that turns the snow
the color the goldenrod
once held. Where three
hills dip in ragged lines,
like a broken bowl
beneath a baby's chair,
a doe has scraped back
snow, then brown leaves,
digging at the earth
for answers. The snow
has picked up, taps
my shoulder, a reminder
that I must get home soon.
Across the hollow, three
barred owls call to one
another, as if the trees
were mirrors, as if sound
were solid, as if what
they said could be seen
in a reflection, the echo
of what I wished
I hadn't said.

Punctuation

The leaves are off, and when we look up
along the ravine, the sky is clear through
a web of limbs. We hike at the bottom
of a dry creek, stones held by the masonry
of mud. My oldest son spies a red-tailed hawk.
It circles out and back over a stand of white oak,
rings we count like children just learning that two
follows one, that three precedes four, that the hunt
leads to the kill.

This morning after church my wife found
a dead chipmunk, throat torn. We didn't
show our boys; instead we dropped its corpse
into the garbage can, lid clanging.

The hawk abandons its fifth arc, flaps
hard, then coasts into an updraft, sailing
toward the ravine just east of us. With its
disappearance, my boys drop their heads,
hunched over searching for loose stones.
I sit on the brown floor, listen to the wind
run the last rust-colored leaves.

Not far off, the knocking of a pileated
woodpecker punctuates the sound that travels
just beneath the world we choose to see.
And in that sound, there is the hammering
and the silence, and finally the ending
we could all too easily miss, even if
we turned away for only a moment.

Blue Song

Walking down the west side of this hill
through maple and beech, you see the river
beyond the river grass, wind blowing along
its top like a child's hand as he waves
goodbye for what promises to be longer
than either of you can imagine. Further
downstream you spy a sandbar: two heron
stalk its edges while at its center huckleberry
bushes loaded with blue bells of fruit wait
to be rung. In the midst of the tall grass, half-
way between forest and river, it's hard to see
anything except the meadow's green slats, sky
and sunlight breaking through to remind you
there is something beyond. You are sure
others have walked here, yet the grass rights
itself so easily that all their paths disappear.
There is no danger. You will not be lost
without water or food; no animal will attack,
no storm will fire and bring down trees
in a tragedy of limbs. As this story ends
you will come to the water's edge, find
a small boat turned over. Out in the river
the current will not be so strong that you
cannot carve it, pull yourself toward the sand-
bar where you will take off your boots, walk
on warm earth at day's end, taste berries that fall
unbidden to your hand—their blue song
like a blessing upon your tongue
given back to the way you have come.

For Ervin Beck

Acknowledgments

Thanks to the following people for their encouragement and advice in the making of these poems and this book: Martha Bates, Lori Bechtel, Ervin Beck, Wendell Berry, Beth Birky, Chris and Brian Black, Andrew and Katie Bode-Lang, Marcia, Bruce, and Dave Bonta, Joyce and Harold Davis, Shelly Davis, Don Flenar, Don and Punky Fox, Keith and Tammy Fynaardt, Dan Gerber, Jim Gorman, Jeff Gundy, Donald Hall, Jim Harrison, William Heyen, Ann Hostetler, Katharine Ings, Virginia Kasamis, Julia Kasdorf, Helen Kiklevich, Don and Melinda Lanham, Mary Linton, Dave Malone, Jim Mellard, Dinty Moore, Erin Murphy, Ray and Laurie Petersen, Lee Peterson, Steve Pett, Jack Ridl, Steve Sherrill, Larry Smith, Lucien Stryk, Mary Swander, Annette Tanner, Jack Troy, Jonathan Watson, Patricia Jabbeh Wesley, Kathy Whitcomb, Rob Wilkins, and Ken Womack.

Many of these poems were finished with the help of generous grants from Penn State University.

My thanks to the editors of the following journals or publications in which these poems first appeared, sometimes in different form.

Aethlon: The Journal of Sport Literature: "Billy Sunday Considers the Second Coming" and "Indiana Love Song"
Appalachia: "Shelter," "Sleep," "Annunciation," "Ars Poetica," and "On the Appalachian Trail, above Delaware Water Gap"
Arts & Letters: "In Praise of Dürer's Dandelions" and "Mid-May in a Year of Early Warmth"

Blueline: "The Movement of Deer," "Just Before Milking," "Adirondack Suite," "At Buttermilk Falls," "Landscape," and "First Snow, after September 11th"

The Christian Science Monitor: "When We Eat"

Epoch: "Learning to Speak the Words"

Evensong: Contemporary Poems of Spirituality (Bottom Dog Press): "Some Heaven," "Amish Gardens," "Prairie Liturgy," "Prayer Requests at a Mennonite Church," and "How Else"

Family Matters: Poems for Our Families (Bottom Dog Press): "Some Heaven" and "How Like the Life"

Farming: "What the Woodchuck Knows" and "This Morning"

Flyway: "Amish Gardens," "Some Heaven," "The Doe," "Near the Center," "After Our Fight," and "Learning to Read"

Fourth River: "First Step"

Front Range Review: "A Father's Notes," "At the Fall Festival," and "At Six I Dream of Dinner with Neil Armstrong"

Gray's Sporting Journal: "Forest Noir"

Green Mountains Review: "Her Time" and "The Way Things Go"

Heartlands: "Propellers"

Image: A Journal of the Arts and Religion: "Penance," "Prayer Requests at a Mennonite Church," and "Nothing More"

The Journal of Kentucky Studies: "The Flowers and Their Fruits"

The Louisville Review: "At the National Gallery Thinking of My Wife"

The Making of Peace: A Poetry Broadside Series (Egress Studio Press): "Trying to Understand the Patriot Act"

The Mennonite: "Prodigal"

Mennonite Quarterly Review: "Blue Song"

The Mid-America Poetry Review: "Once Again"

The Midwest Quarterly: "The Possibility of Rain"

North American Review: "The Certainty of Weight"

Poetry East: "Aftermath," "A Lesson in Mercy from My Wife, on the Last Day of May," and "Saint Francis Preaches to the Birds"

Quarterly West: "Resurrection, or What He Told Me to Do When He Died"

Rattle: "Tattoo"

Rhubarb: "At the Fall Festival" and "Illusion"

River Styx: "A Country Lost"

Rough Place Plain: Poems of the Mountains (Salt Marsh Pottery Press): "While We Wait for Spring"

Southern Indiana Review: "Father's Hands"

The Sow's Ear Poetry Review: "Spelling Test"

Sudden Stories: A Mammoth Anthology of Minuscule Fiction (Mammoth Press): "The Beginning of the Story"

Tundra: "Meditation on the South Skunk River"

TODD DAVIS teaches creative writing, environmental studies, and American literature at Penn State University–Altoona. His poems have been nominated for the Pushcart Prize and have appeared in such journals and magazines as *The North American Review, The Christian Science Monitor, River Styx, Arts & Letters, Quarterly West, Green Mountains Review, Poetry East, Many Mountains Moving, Natural Bridge, Epoch, Rattle, The Louisville Review, The Nebraska Review, The Midwest Quarterly, The Red Cedar Review,* and *Image: A Journal of the Arts and Religion.* In September 2002, his first book of poems, *Ripe,* was published by Bottom Dog Press. Some of the poems from *Ripe* are anthologized in *A Cappella: Mennonite Voices in Poetry* (University of Iowa Press, 2003) and in *Visiting Frost: Poems Inspired by the Life and Work of Robert Frost* (University of Iowa Press, 2005).